What Is a Family?

What Is a Family?

Elaine Moore
Illustrated by
Patricia Mattozzi

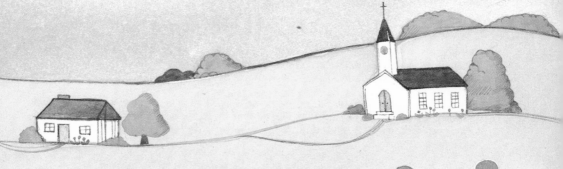

Publishing House
St. Louis

Library of Congress Cataloging-in-Publication Data

Moore, Elaine.
    What is a family?

    Summary: Describes different types of families, such as those with step- and half-relationships, adoptions, deaths, or no children at all; and emphasizes the commitment we must make to family members and to God.
    1. Family—United States—Juvenile literature.   2. Family—United States—Religious life—Juvenile literature.   [1. Family. 2. Christian life]   I. Title.
HQ536.M56   1987   306.8'5   87-5237
ISBN 0-570-04171-6

1 2 3 4 5 6 7 8 9 10 DP 96 95 94 93 92 91 90 89 88 87

To Mom and Dad,
Diane and Nick

What is a family? You know who belongs in your family. Perhaps your family has a mother, father, sister, and brother. But does a family have to have all those people?

Mickey's family doesn't. Mickey has a
stepfather and a mother, two stepsisters, three
stepbrothers, one natural sister and one natural
brother—and one baby half-brother everybody
takes turns holding. When Mickey's family sits
down to eat, a lot of people fold their hands
in prayer.

Mark doesn't have any brothers or sisters. He doesn't even have a daddy anymore. His daddy died. Mark's family is just Mark and his mother. Last Sunday Mark took a picture of his dad to Sunday school. His friends all said, "Hey, you look just like your dad."

Does that mean people have to look alike to be a family? They don't in Emily's family. Emily's parents weren't able to have children of their own, so they adopted Emily and her brothers and sisters. Her family has people of many shapes and sizes.

Do people have to live in the same house to be a family? They don't in Tanya's family. Her older sister lives at college, and her older brother lives by himself in an apartment. Tanya hardly ever sees her brother or sister—except for Christmas, when everybody comes home and they all squeeze into one car and go to church together.

Do people have to have children in the house to be a family? Not at the Watson house. Mr. and Mrs. Watson never had any children, nor even any adopted ones. But Mr. and Mrs. Watson still thank God for being a family.

So, what is a family?

It doesn't have to be children and parents—or stepparents. The people don't have to look alike or live in the same house. There don't have to be any children either.

So, what is a family?

Here's a clue:
God the Father loves us as a father.
Jesus, His Son, loves us as a brother.
The Holy Spirit gave us faith in Jesus and
made us part of God's family.

God promised that love long ago when He promised a Savior to the first family, Adam and Eve.

That's the clue: Promise.

Families start with a special promise
between a man and a woman. They promise to
love and care for each other as long as
they live.

They also promise to love and care for any children they might have, however they get them.

That man and woman also promise to help their children learn to make the same promise of love and care for each person in the family.

Your parents promised that to each other and to God. And God promised to help them give that love and care to their family.

Your parents have helped you learn to promise love and care for your family. You can say that promise out loud, or you can say it softly.

You can say "I love you" to your mother and father. You can say "I love you" to your sister and brother. Even to your aunts and uncles and grandpas and grandmas.

And you can promise your love for a long, long time.